PEOPLE IN MY NEIGHBORHOOD

THE CHEF

Jared Siemens

LIGHTBOX
openlightbox.com

Go to
www.openlightbox.com
and enter this book's
unique code.

ACCESS CODE

LBXK7953

Lightbox is an all-inclusive digital solution for the teaching and learning of curriculum topics in an original, groundbreaking way. Lightbox is based on National Curriculum Standards.

OPTIMIZED FOR

- ✓ **TABLETS**
- ✓ **WHITEBOARDS**
- ✓ **COMPUTERS**
- ✓ **AND MUCH MORE!**

STANDARD FEATURES OF LIGHTBOX

AUDIO High-quality narration using text-to-speech system

VIDEOS Embedded high-definition video clips

ACTIVITIES Printable PDFs that can be emailed and graded

WEBLINKS Curated links to external, child-safe resources

SLIDESHOWS Pictorial overviews of key concepts

INTERACTIVE MAPS Interactive maps and aerial satellite imagery

QUIZZES Ten multiple choice questions that are automatically graded and emailed for teacher assessment

KEY WORDS Matching key concepts to their definitions

VIDEOS

WEBLINKS

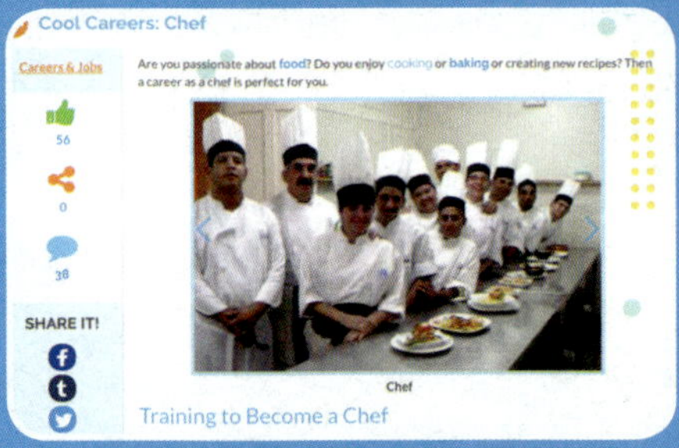

SLIDESHOWS

QUIZZES

PEOPLE IN MY NEIGHBORHOOD

THE CHEF

CONTENTS

There are many different people in my neighborhood.

The chef is a person in my neighborhood.

A chef works at a restaurant.

San Francisco had seven top-rated restaurants in 2018. This is more than any other city in the United States.

A restaurant is a place where people go to eat a meal.

The head chef is in charge of everything in the kitchen.

He tells the other chefs what meals they will make.

Chefs know what foods taste good together. This helps them make new dishes.

They know how to make many healthy meals by memory.

People in the United States eat about **100 acres** (40 hectares) of pizza each day. That is about **350 slices** each second.

A chef uses many tools in the kitchen. His knife is a very important tool.

He uses it to cut up vegetables and meat.

The chef cooks food on a hot stove.

There are more than **1 million restaurants** in the United States.

She has to watch it closely so that it does not burn.

Chefs wash their hands and keep their kitchens clean.

This keeps germs away from the food.

The chef puts the food on a plate in a special way.

He wants it to look nice for the customers.

Chefs are important people in my neighborhood.

More than **145,000 people** work as chefs or head cooks in the **United States**.

See what you have learned about the chef.

Describe what you see in each of the pictures.

KEY WORDS

Research has shown that as much as 65 percent of all written material published in English is made up of 300 words. These 300 words cannot be taught using pictures or learned by sounding them out. They must be recognized by sight. This book contains 74 common sight words to help young readers improve their reading fluency and comprehension. This book also teaches young readers several important content words, such as proper nouns. These words are paired with pictures to aid in learning and improve understanding.

Page	Sight Words First Appearance
4	are, different, in, many, my, people, there
5	a, is, the
6	any, at, city, had, more, other, states, than, this, works
7	eat, go, place, to, where
8	head, of
9	he, make, tells, they, what, will
10	foods, good, helps, know, new, them, together
11	about, by, day, each, how, second, that
12	his, important, uses, very
13	and, cut, it, up
14	on
15	does, has, not, she, so, watch
16	hands, keep, their
17	away, from
18	puts, way
19	for, look, wants
21	as, or

Page	Content Words First Appearance
4	neighborhood
5	chef, person
6	restaurant, San Francisco, United States
7	meal
8	head chef, kitchen
10	dishes
11	memory, pizza, slices
12	knife, tools
13	meat, vegetables
14	stove
17	germs
18	plate
19	customers
21	head cooks

Published by Smartbook Media Inc.
350 5th Avenue, 59th Floor New York, NY 10118
Website: www.openlightbox.com

Library of Congress Control Number: 2018930449

ISBN 978-1-5105-3827-6 (hardcover)
ISBN 978-1-5105-3828-3 (multi-user eBook)

032018
120117

Printed in Brainerd, Minnesota, United States
1 2 3 4 5 6 7 8 9 0 22 21 20 19 18

Project Coordinator: Jared Siemens
Designer: Nick Newton

Every reasonable effort has been made to trace ownership and to obtain permission to reprint copyright material. The publisher would be pleased to have any errors or omissions brought to its attention so that they may be corrected in subsequent printings.

The publisher acknowledges Alamy, Shutterstock, Getty Images, and iStock as its primary image suppliers for this title.